GROWING GARDENS

Pollinator Gardens

BY SAMANTHA S. BELL

An Imprint of Abdo Publishing
abdobooks.com

abdobooks.com

Published by Abdo Publishing, a division of ABDO, PO Box 398166, Minneapolis, Minnesota 55439.

Printed in the United States of America, North Mankato, Minnesota.
052025
092025

Cover Photo: Sander Meertins Photography/Shutterstock Images
Interior Photos: Amine Chakour/Shutterstock Images, 4–5; Shutterstock Images, 7, 9, 14, 18, 25, 28 (top), 29 (bottom); Jennifer Dunn Photography/Shutterstock Images, 10; filmstudio/E+/Getty Images, 12–13; Ami Parikh/Shutterstock Images, 17; iStockphoto, 20–21; Clare Gainey/Alamy, 22; Jasonfang/E+/Getty Images, 23; Cathy Keifer/Shutterstock Images, 26; Pelevina Ksinia/Shutterstock Images, 28 (bottom); Patrick Jennings/Shutterstock Images, 29 (top)

Editor: Christa Kelly
Series Designer: Katharine Hale

Library of Congress Control Number: 2024948988

Publisher's Cataloging-in-Publication Data

Names: Bell, Samantha S., author.
Title: Pollinator gardens / by Samantha S. Bell
Description: Minneapolis, Minnesota: Abdo Publishing, 2026 | Series: Growing gardens | Includes online resources and index.
Identifiers: ISBN 9781098297428 (lib. bdg.) | ISBN 9798384919940 (ebook)
Subjects: LCSH: Gardens--Juvenile literature. | Gardening--Juvenile literature. | Plant-pollinator relationships--Juvenile literature. | Horticulture--Juvenile literature.
Classification: DDC 635.9--dc23

CONTENTS

CHAPTER 1
Feasting on Flowers 4

CHAPTER 2
Planning a Pollinator Garden 12

CHAPTER 3
Growing Pollinator Plants 20

Garden Plants 28
Glossary 30
Online Resources 31
Learn More 31
Index 32
About the Author 32

Hummingbirds use their long tongues and thin beaks to reach nectar deep in flowers.

CHAPTER 1

Feasting on Flowers

Kara watched as a tiny hummingbird flitted around the bird feeder. Her mom put out the feeder every spring. Kara wondered what the bird ate the rest of the year. She asked her mom what hummingbirds ate when they didn't have the feeder.

Her mom explained that they gather **nectar** from flowers.

Kara asked, "Can I grow flowers for the hummingbirds?"

"That's a great idea," said her mom. "You can grow a pollinator garden. It will provide food for hummingbirds, butterflies, and bees."

Kara chose a sunny spot along the fence for her garden. Then Kara and her mom went to a gardening store. Kara looked at all the beautiful flowering plants. She chose plants that grew naturally in their area.

Kara planted the flowers in her garden. Suddenly, a hummingbird whirred by. Kara was glad her garden would provide food for so many creatures.

Planting pollinator-friendly plants can attract beautiful birds and butterflies to gardens.

Providing for Pollinators

Pollination helps plants **reproduce**. Pollination occurs when pollen from the male part of a flower reaches the female part of a flower. This allows seeds to grow.

Some plants can pollinate themselves. Other plants rely on the wind to carry their pollen.

Powerful Pollinators

Many people know that bees, butterflies, and hummingbirds are pollinators. But other animals also act as pollinators. These animals include moths, wasps, beetles, and flies. Bats are pollinators too. In some countries, lizards, geckos, and skinks also pollinate flowers.

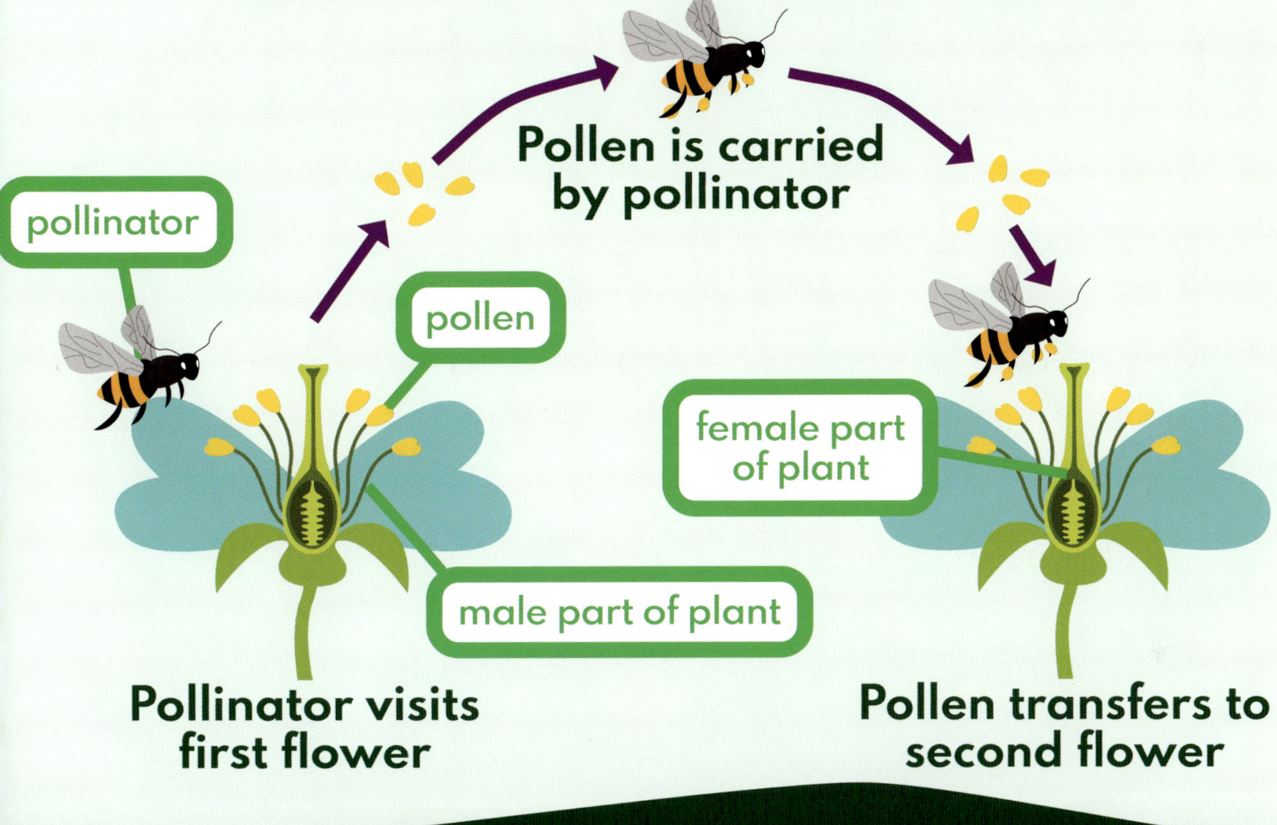

Animals such as bees, butterflies, birds, and bats pollinate plants by transferring pollen between flowers.

But many plants need pollinators. These are animals that carry pollen. Many insects and birds are pollinators. Without pollinators, many crops could not grow. Pollinators help produce 75 percent of people's food.

From 2004 to 2024, the number of monarch butterflies decreased by 90 percent.

Pollinators are very important. But in many places, their **habitats** are being destroyed. Natural areas where pollinators live are being replaced by houses, stores, and roads. The plants that pollinators eat are removed.

Without food and shelter, many pollinators are dying.

People can help pollinators by creating pollinator gardens. These gardens have plants that attract pollinators. Some are plants that provide them with food. Others give them shelter. By helping pollinators, gardeners can support the whole **ecosystem**.

Further Evidence

Look at the website below. Does it give any new evidence to support Chapter One?

Build a Butterfly Garden

abdocorelibrary.com/pollinator-gardens

There are dozens of pollinator plants for gardeners to choose from.

CHAPTER 2

Planning a Pollinator Garden

The first step in planning a pollinator garden is deciding where to grow the plants. Many people grow pollinator gardens in sunny areas. Butterflies and other pollinators like to rest in the sun. Many flowering plants also grow best with a lot of sunlight.

Pollinator gardens can take up whole yards or just a few pots.

Some gardeners plant pollinator gardens in sunny parts of yards. Others put pollinator plants in containers on balconies, porches, and patios. Flowering vines can be grown on **trellises** if there is not much room.

Plants for Pollinators

Once a gardener has chosen a location for their garden, they can decide which plants to grow. The best plants for pollinator gardens are native plants. These are plants that have naturally grown in an area for a long time. These plants provide food and shelter for an area's pollinators. Native plants also tend to be stronger. They grow well in the area's **climate**.

Invasive Species

Invasive species are kinds of plants that are not native to an area. These plants take water, nutrients, and growing room from native plants. This can hurt native plants and their pollinators. Invasive species should not be planted in pollinator gardens.

This means the plants do not need as much care.

When choosing plants, gardeners should think about how much space they have. Some plants need only a little space. These plants include many types of flowers. They can be grown in containers. Other plants need lots of space. These plants include fruit trees.

The best pollinator gardens have a wide variety of plants. Choosing a variety of plants helps attract different types of pollinators. Different pollinators need different types of plants. Some plants have flowers shaped like long tubes. These plants include cardinal flowers, honeysuckles, and columbines. These flowers attract butterflies, moths,

Experts recommend that people grow perennial plants in their pollinator gardens. These plants come back every year.

and hummingbirds. Some plants have round or flat flowers. These plants include phlox, marigolds, milkweeds, and sunflowers. These flowers attract bees, flies, and beetles.

Some pollinators eat leaves rather than nectar or pollen. Caterpillars grow into butterflies and moths. They eat the leaves of carrot, parsley, and dill plants. People can grow these plants in pollinator gardens too.

Pussy willows bloom in the late winter and early spring. They provide pollen for bees when few other flowers are blooming.

Growing different plants also helps pollinators find food throughout the growing season. Many pollinators feed from a single area for most of the year. People can help by choosing plants that bloom during different seasons. This provides food for pollinators throughout the year.

Primary Source

Shaun Booth is the co-author of a gardening book and owns a gardening company. He said:

> Almost any property is suitable for a pollinator garden, no matter the size, shape, growing conditions, or location. . . . With the right approach, a pollinator garden can be grown in the toughest of conditions including clay soil, dry shade, and tough **urban** sites.

Jaime Gold. "Why You Might Want to Add a Pollinator Garden to Your Home Space." *Forbes*, 13 Aug. 2024, forbes.com. Accessed 31 Oct. 2024.

Comparing Texts

Does this quote support the information in this chapter? Or does it give a different perspective?

Different plants should be planted at different times of year.

CHAPTER 3

Growing Pollinator Plants

Once the garden is planned, it's time to get growing! Some gardeners start by planting seeds. Others start with plants that have already sprouted. Sprouted plants cost more than seeds, but they take less time to grow.

Some people plant seeds in outdoor containers during the winter. The seeds sprout when the weather warms.

Gardeners who grow plants from seeds should start their gardens early. People should plant seeds during the fall or winter before the growing season. This gives the seeds time to sprout. Seeds planted in the fall should be covered with soil. Seeds planted in late winter can be scattered over the snow. The sun will warm up the seeds. It will also melt the snow. This provides the seeds with water so they can grow.

Sunflower seeds can be planted after the last frost.

People planting sprouted plants can start their gardens in the spring. The plants will bloom during the growing season. People can dig a small hole in the soil for each plant. Then they can cover the roots with soil.

Growing plants in groups or clusters makes them easier for pollinators to spot. It also allows the pollinators to feed more easily. They can go quickly from flower to flower.

Caring for the Garden

Gardeners should regularly check on their gardens to make sure they are healthy. They should water their plants. New plants need

Homes for Pollinators

Pollinators need places to live. People can provide them with nesting sites in their gardens. Branches and rock piles make good homes for pollinators. Dead garden plants can also provide shelter for pollinators during the winter.

Plants should be watered at their bases. Then the plants' roots can drink the water.

more water than plants that are already growing. Plants also need more water when there is not much rain. Native plants do not need as much water as non-native plants. Gardeners should water plants when the soil is dry.

Chemicals that kill weeds are called herbicides. Some herbicides kill pollinator plants such as milkweed.

Weeding is another way to keep gardens healthy. Weeds take water and nutrients away from garden plants. Tall weeds can also block sunlight. Some stores sell chemicals to kill weeds. But these can harm pollinators.

Instead of using chemicals, people should pull weeds up by the roots.

Pollinator gardens add bright color to yards, patios, and porches. These gardens provide pollinators with food and shelter. They play an important part in keeping ecosystems healthy.

Explore Online

Visit the website below. Does it give any new information about pollinator gardens that wasn't in Chapter Three?

Planting for Pollinators

abdocorelibrary.com/pollinator-gardens

Garden Plants

Milkweed

There are about 100 types of milkweed native to North America. Monarch butterflies lay their eggs on the plant's leaves. When the caterpillars hatch, they eat the leaves.

Phlox

Phlox is native to parts of the eastern, midwestern, and southern United States. It forms small, brightly colored flowers. It provides food for bees, butterflies, and hummingbirds.

Cardinal flower

Cardinal flowers are native to parts of the United States and eastern Canada. The plants are tall with red flowers. They provide food for hummingbirds.

Sunflower

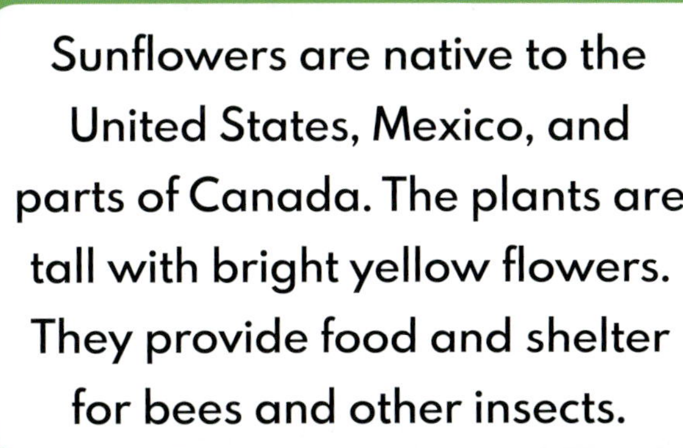

Sunflowers are native to the United States, Mexico, and parts of Canada. The plants are tall with bright yellow flowers. They provide food and shelter for bees and other insects.

Glossary

climate
an area with specific weather patterns

ecosystem
a community of living and non-living things interacting together

habitats
the natural homes of plants or animals

nectar
a sugary liquid that plants make to attract pollinators

reproduce
to make more of something

trellises
frames that support climbing plants as they grow

urban
describing a city

Online Resources

To learn more about growing pollinator gardens, visit our free resource websites below.

Visit **abdocorelibrary.com** or scan this QR code for free Common Core resources for teachers and students, including vetted activities, multimedia, and booklinks, for deeper subject comprehension.

Visit **abdobooklinks.com** or scan this QR code for free additional online weblinks for further learning. These links are routinely monitored and updated to provide the most current information available.

Learn More

Daniels, Jaret C. *Pollinators & Native Plants for Kids: An Introduction to Botany.* Adventure, 2025.

Wilson, Libby. *Flower Gardens.* Abdo, 2026.

World of Pollinators. Fox Chapel, 2023.

Index

cardinal flowers, 16
carrots, 17
columbines, 16

dill, 17

garden care, 24–27

honeysuckles, 16

marigolds, 17
milkweeds, 17

parsley, 17
phlox, 17
planning, 6, 13–19
planting, 6, 21–24
pollinators, 5–11, 13, 15–18, 24, 26–27

sunflowers, 17

About the Author

Samantha S. Bell lives in the foothills of the Blue Ridge Mountains with her family and four cats. She has written more than 150 nonfiction books for students in kindergarten through high school. She loves watching the pollinators that visit her flowers.